This Town

This Town
Poems of Correspondence

Kyle Laws & Jared Smith

Liquid Light Press

Premium Chapbook First Edition

Copyright © 2017

ISBN-10: 0-9985487-0-7

ISBN-13: 978-0-9985487-0-8

Liquid Light Press

poetry for the heart

www.liquidlightpress.com

Book and cover design by M. D. Friedman

Contents

Jared Smith

How Do You Look at This Space?

Growing old I write colder in fire,
more to lose and therefore words are golden
fleece, are the sacred ark of the covenant,
the vessel of the blood which is eternal life,
the mythology of which insanity is formed,
the vessel which is the craft that poets study,
abandoning it in the years when flesh is young
and dying before reconciling themselves to
becoming the deserts that surround them. You
have not read many poems like this in academia.

I open fewer visions into the meanings than I
used to when sitting in barrooms with high strung girls
because no seduction is needed, no love will save me
except any part of my soul that will escape the flesh,
and I have little hope of that since science is science.
I look instead to solid things that have had meaning.

I look to the structures we have surrounded ourselves
with, to the hallowed weathered boards we have formed
our structures with, the stores, the homes, the factories,
the dreams still undefined which we have lost in time,
our families, our children, our schoolyard memories,
the space that we have encircled in time to call ours.

I give it a key, and I hold it out to you, to open what.

One could say it is a box in time,
a cubicle spanning the space of stars
as the world goes on its uncharted way,
and there are many ways to get inside

but for a certain fee you get a metal key
opening doors to your child's future,
to the desks where college applications
will go whistling across the country and
dropping down on institutional blotters,
or maybe where you will be sitting when
the cancer that gets you comes calling,
but what is important is what's in it now
because the seeds of everything are here,

so you put the key into its lock and there are
books on shelves that lead back into the room
and maybe there are words on the pages you
haven't read yet or perhaps you have forgotten
and it might be this is the foyer of your frame house
and it might be that this is more of a used book shop
located between a diner at the corner of Main
and a Great Clips barber shop, a hardware store
on the other side, a coffee shop or odds and ends
that change from year to year as owners fade,
but each word remembers its author's voice
and page on page each book chants its harmony
and thank goodness the books go back and back,

because when you look at the key as it lies
on the front desk near the cash register, and
you pull back, it becomes a part of the town
where you live in a vast uncomprehending maze
that matches the mountains' and valleys' complexity
as you pull back farther on your Google maps
and the building you own the key for disappears,
and once again, how do you look at this space?
I could go on and on but only with your presence.

This Town

This town lives in a snapshot from a box camera.
It is not my town. It may not be yours.
It exists at the back of your mind.
A town you travel through on a cross country trip.
Someplace you stop for coffee in the middle of the night.
Its name is Town. But who lives in a town called Town?

A woman in a red house on a bluff over the sea.
A tall hedge surrounds the house.
No one paints a house red.
You could only acquire it from generations before
as the hedge you can barely see over.
Awnings shutter the porch so you cannot see in.

Why would you want to see in?
There is nothing missing in your past.
But you want a future different from the one you see.
There is confidence in a woman who would live
in a red house. A confidence you want for yourself.
A language you want to learn to speak.

Jared Smith

The Night Marchers

There are certain streets you don't walk down,
streets where half the lights are blown out and
shadows warm their hands around old oil cans,
places where the street is just too narrow, too
closely guarded by dry graffitied sliding doors
so seldom seen the signs might mean anything.

These are the streets college students ignore
going to and from late night classroom lectures,
the streets that even taxi drivers stay away from
and homeless people tell of the darkness that waits
and of the muted crying they hear at midnight.
They are where bones are discovered at dawn.

Not that you have ever been there. You have
passed with a nervous glance back into the shadows,
perhaps have tightened your fist around your keys
so that one key protrudes like a switchblade knife
between the cold fingers clenched within your pocket
and you hurry back toward the artificial lights.

Sometimes lying awake before the night recedes
you can hear the dreadful roar of universes clashing
perhaps coming from these corners of the city and
you say as you wake it is the garbage trucks coming,
clanging and banging, barging their way through,
sweeping away the mountains of debris we build,
and sometimes it is, but that's only what you think.

It is the same in each city, as the police records indicate,
there are the unsolved mysteries and murders, the lost
mostly sequestered together down these darkened lanes
near where the heavy tankers come in by warehouses.
And it's true too in the small forgotten midwest towns
where along one dusty lane a farmer's home has gone to dust,
his family disappeared within the holes that line the house,
that house that even small children stay away from now,
the cage now keeping something in and something out
while people sleep and beings from other dimensions enter
perhaps as dreams and perhaps as something else entirely.

Jared Smith

Watching What Needs Watching on the Highway,

I'm wavering between 70 and 75 somewhere
past Exit 135 heading down toward Town
with the external temperature painting lakes
shimmering above the distant point that concrete
makes at the end of desert highways between cacti,
and I jiggle the plastic dial to keep my radio station tuned,
trying to keep myself awake in this metal cloth-skinned
creature that runs itself on the speed of extinct plant life
past the signs for fast food and gas and topless girls
and mileage signs that skirt the edges of vision

and what we have to keep track of, you and I,
are the bright red arrows and lights on the dashboard
with their pictures of thermometers and dipsticks
and headlights and half-empty markers all lit up,
as well as the black and white cruisers behind signs
and the unmarked cars that have antennae far too long,
just those things, the same things we find on every road.
That's what we carry with us always, and it's boring
as painted turtles but it's what keeps us alive watching.

Maybe I start thinking about painted turtles then, moving
heavily from their burrows in mirage beyond the painted desert,
and of jack rabbits gray as ghosts among the dry grasses,
of all the shining minds that I have passed on this road,
of the children in their boxes, the fathers off to war,
when the car crests a slight rise in the road and leaps
airborne briefly outside a house bright red in memory,
then down into the scream of machinery separating from flesh
and flesh separating from machinery eyes wide open sudden
come to rest one way or another at last and starting to wake
where one belongs in time beneath the sky.

Kyle Laws

At the Crest, There Is No Wait

after the drawbridge swung sideways for the last time,
not for passage of a tall ship, but for the antennae of navigation,
the sounding of fish. They come to Town for the angling,

waters once plied by whalers out of Long Island, by pirates
who lured craft onto shoals, the storms out of nowhere,
out of the last call at taprooms.

Here at the crossing gate——a slow wait,
radio left on as the ignition sits between start and off
so you can sing to an airborne leap you will not take.

You will not leave the car for a canal you could swim across
as the tender rotates the gear for the swing of wooden buttress,
the complex cross of beams stared up at

before boats were buried in front yards,
before the men of Town left for the Coast Guard,
before women's work became an Atlantic City chorus line.

Inside the Glass Front Doors

The golden retriever is almost a fixture
beneath a corner table in the back of the cafe,
sprawled out and with tongue lolling, taking
everything in lying on the floor half asleep,
but with head raised between an old man's legs.
He catalogues the day the way that dogs do,
the people coming in through open doors and closed,
the way the eggs come in each morning from the back
with the rancid, titillating smell of chickens
and how those that eat them come in the front.
How the bacon comes in with another man formed
around the full bodied smell of pigs and grains.
The chicken man has grains too. Perhaps grain is
somehow drawn to the back doorway, the worn
wood doorway with paint chipped off. He faces
toward the food-way. But he takes in the rest,
and hears the car too fast down Main Street,
the rattling of machinery, whoop of sirens,
smells the sea that surrounds us all and dozes
knowing lying between his man's legs all is well,
and that the woman who brings food will come
and each plate will carry easy over eggs and toast
and that cups of coffee will slowly light each table
and a bottomless pan of water will appear as it does.
He has no names for these things but knows them
as every creature, every part of Town, knows itself.

A fly comes in off one of the old fishing boats
harbored days away and says meaningless about his ears.
Dog raises a paw and kicks his head, and the fly goes on
about his business one plate of food at a time, its eyes
seeing the way that the eyes of flies see in multitudes
so that each person coming in to eat at Mom's Cafe
brings maybe a thousand more with him, all the same
bringing food in the backdoor and taking it out the front
and smiling with teeth that could take your wings off
while handing life to each other on old chipped plates.
It's Sunday morning, but that doesn't mean much:
The whole town comes by in multitudes each day
as sun begins to bake the pavements hot outside,
and the coffee grinder mimics the sound of all machines
in so many dimensions that a fly cannot keep track.
It's okay because life goes on with wings on a full belly
and one doesn't suppose anyone sees anything really
but ghosts and shadows and metal cash registers
and the dry soil still speaking of Dust Bowl memories
and little Towns and Urban Centers
and something that is bigger than dogs or old men
or even memories that keep right on filling their days.

When I First Came to Town, the Only Business

besides a small grocery store was the turkey farm,
squawk heard all the way down to the bay of oysters.

No reason to call it other than Town, where
you went for what you didn't grow or raise or mill.

Someone tried a café and bar on the north side,
converted Robert Edmunds' house,

back section paneled not with plaster and lath,
but sheathing of white cedar from the swamp,

the grove where Robert went to pray.
"No better place," he said, "not limited to Sundays."

Why Would Anyone Want to Live in Town?

Driving one day, taking a detour off Delsea Drive
onto a dirt road not far from the bay,
small paths appeared. I took one on foot.
Trees thinned, an inhale and exhale
as if the forest were breathing as it opened up,
the waves a small belly, a girl not yet a woman.
I knew I wanted to live there.

Sarah Matthews opened the door not far
from Fishing Creek School, two rooms and a bell.
"We don't sell to outsiders," she said.

I told her about the tide lines littered with mussels
and clams, seaweed and kelp, and glass in green
and blue and purple hues. No umbrellas. No bathers.

"How do you feel about cows?
They've gotten unruly since my husband's been gone."
I didn't know if she meant Philadelphia or passed on.
"There's a fishing shack not far from the water,
not far from where the cattle have gravitated.
It's red, can't miss it. Take this road beside the house,"
road, an exaggeration.

Jared Smith

The Salt Marshes

Beyond the doctors' offices, real estate brokers, greasy diners,
beyond the houses, there were the salt marshes themselves
shifting back and forth, waving on all sides outside the town filled
with the smell of stranded fish and overabundance of clams,
broken shells, sandworms, bloodworms, fiddler crabs,
and the steel gray of herons wading waiting in the evening
knowing that from this flatness one could pluck flashes of silver
and carry them off into the sunset as if they had never been.

I got to know those marshes, as I knew the heavy smell of horses
that came to permeate my clothes, though they were not water horses
and had to be left tied to the bones of cypress knees at the end of the beach
when I wanted to wander halfway inland and roll up my pant legs, feel
the earth oozing up between my toes as I walked to the inner island,
more a raised sandbar than an island, but with vegetation, a tree
where ospreys landed in the daytime and a great horned owl at night,
where the bones of fish and rodents lay scattered in a bleached heap,
perhaps the leftovers of meals or the beginnings of land or both.

When the wind howled from the ocean or Town itself grew too close,
when the wizened stub fingered fishermen drank too much at the bar
and began bragging of all the things they had dredged from their nets
as the moon rose in the evening those marshes would be my shelter,
and I would walk out into them beneath the blank eyes of the owl,
and I would know that the grasses had eyes and the soil itself a soul.
This was separate from where I lived, of course, but it was there
contained within the rib cage of a vessel that knew the night unafraid.

How Can You Afford to Live in Town?

I dance in a chorus line in Atlantic City in summer.
Sarah doesn't charge much for the shack,
glad for the company.

A dual life. I don't talk about either with the other.
No way the Town people would understand.
But it gives me winter, fall, and spring to myself.
Me and the cows. And I keep a horse in a corral
between shack and dunes.

And if you don't run too many cattle,
the dunes give enough feed for a horse or two,
something the old timers figured out.

The cost of feed came up in conversation
the other night when Sarah had me over for dinner,
eating what I took as chicken until she asked
what I thought and got that look on her face
I have come to know as mischievous.

I remembered the rabbit cages out back of her house.
Another *I will never* down the drain.
Atlantic City not the only temptress, but Town too.

Demanding for a Dancer to Keep in Shape in Town

Certainly no studios with mirrors on the walls,
but walking, riding the horse, chopping wood,
washing blankets by hand and hanging on the line
when no wind blows—they all help. In front
of the fire, I keep hamstrings loose by stretching,
nowhere to dance except narrow taproom floors.

Few hike the trails off the curve of Fulling Mill
that connects to Delsea Drive. The paths of deer
are so worn in the sandy soil, the undergrowth
will never spring back as they head every day
to Fishing Mill Stream.

I know their habits, routes, follow as if hunting,
not with rifle, but with the thrill of being wild,
in tune, bending my head to drink from the cedar
stained stream. The mill that once fulled the wool
of sheep—ramshackle, only the road through woods
with its name still used. Sun slants on the wheel
as the wide-racked buck that leads this group
disappears into the dense of trees.

Jared Smith

The Owner of Windows

Names are tricky.
The cafe owner's name is Dawn
and she is a window into a world
that never was and was more than 40 years gone.
She is the only woman in Town who remembers Danny
from the age of 12 tending nets until he went off to Vietnam
leaving her pregnant with the sea his last night at home,
leaving her with something shapeless that never came right.

But that's long gone now. It's all out of the box,
and each morning you can see her impassive features
looking out over Main Street behind the plate glass
with the foot-high white letters spelling Open At Dawn
in an arch over her face, and you can see yourself
reflected back from the early sun imposed on herself
surrounded by rosebuds, silverware and cash register.

And Dawn is seeing you the same way, transposed
across her face and the faces of Danny and his brother
in the years before his brother bought the service station
which is the last thing you pass leaving any town you come to.
The names stick in her mind, and they're tricky.
She isn't young and Danny is as far away as the sun itself.

That's about as close to mirrors on the wall I come to here,
learning to see myself in the eyes of those who have seen the dead,
learning to balance my art with the rosebuds and cash registers,
not really knowing the names but more the suppleness of form
that people carry with them at dawn and then again at evening.
I like to think that it is this studying of form and history and
this long, long act of loving that will eventually imbue my dance
and take back to the boardwalk something that will illuminate us
and will place me center stage in a place of my own. It should.

Kyle Laws

Danny's Café or Breakfast in Town

Danny runs the café at the edge of Town.
It has another name but no one calls it that.
You can get scrapple there, a Philadelphia delicacy
from parts of the pig no one wants to think about,
sausage with a dusty flavor. You put lots of ketchup
on it. I never acquired the taste.

Or there is pork roll on thin Italian bread
with cheese and scrambled eggs. That I like.
But mostly it's the potatoes on the grill from the time
Danny opens until he scrapes it clean for lunch.
Huge mounds of potatoes that he scoops out
of the bucket where they soak. When potato water
hits the grill and sizzles and the skins begin to flake
and he mixes in onions and sweet peppers,
you can smell it all over the café of seven booths,
four tables, and a counter.

No matter how tired you are from the night before,
you try to get there before he pulls them off for lunch,
sometimes heading out without a shower,
just a quick brush of teeth at the sink, pulling back
your hair into a twist or wrapping it up in a bandana.

Jared Smith

Turner Bay

Late autumn and the sea is the color and turbulence of sky—
rolling into each other at the horizon, but that's only the beginning.
The sea goes on down to a darkness where life lives on sulfur,
and the economy has gone to hell. The dance stage is empty
so often I've taken to staying home, walking the beach all day
swinging a metal detector back and forth over the sands,
counting the air bubbles blown by clams beneath my feet,
brushing aside the drying seaweed and fiddler crabs fiddling
while my skin burns and the trawlers stay in port peeling paint.

A bad job of it. I found four dimes a quarter eleven pennies
and an old Coast Guard medal with its ribbon eaten away.
Not much for a living hunting for pirate gold this way. Better
though than driving miles of concrete highway on a dream,
and the IRS won't take this away from me. Another 3/4 of a dollar
plus one penny and I jingle as I walk in the wind like castanets
beneath the moon on a dead man's ferry with Lorca's pirate ships.

A mist of sand and salt fills every pore of my skin, every day
of my life, my clothes, the windows along the main street of Town,
the bottle of cheap home-brew in my father's rusted Ford, the
song of Louis' trumpet coming from an iPod in the pawn shop
by the Off Her Rocker antique store which will sell you anything
for the memories of people who have gone away and won't return.

I know it's time to be getting on again, hitting the road, because
in this town if you don't move they paint you and put you in a frame.
A town, like the people within it, is defined as much by what is
   outside.
I think of The Painted Desert where every livid color is set in stone.

The Depression in Town

Nobody paid much attention to October 1929.
Who had invested in New York?
There wasn't an easy way to get there,
not over land, and sea-going was worse—
you had to breach the Atlantic coast.

Most of our dollars passed from hand to hand.
You knew the winter folk, if not by name, by face.
Someone should just set up one big book and record
the buys and sells, a bartering system not requiring
equal exchange, settle up between ourselves at the end
of summer after all the tourist money flowed in.

I proposed the scheme at Town meeting.
It took until 1933 for us to even talk about it.
Everyone just kept thinking it was a spell of bad luck
that would turn, the good coming back like a tide.
The old men asked what we'd do about the new folks,
the ones stranded, no place else to go.
What did they contribute? What did they have to sell?
"We grow or fish or raise, send any excess up north
to markets on wharves in Camden and Philadelphia.
We just have to get through the winters.
The banks can't be trusted anymore."

Because I lived with Sarah—how they referred to it,
not in the same house, but to them it was the same
because it was her land—they said go ahead,
if you think you can keep it straight, give it a try.
This wasn't trust. They just knew if I botched it
they'd work it out among themselves, their memories
as long as the wait for the summer tourists to return.

Jared Smith

That Night in '41

It was their eyes that always got me,
flat and unblinking as dinner plates
or as the coins we traded in markets,
but come from the deep with something
horrible endless dredged up to the light,
to be thrown dead naked on dinner plates.
You eat what you can get, I know, but
the scales themselves catch in your throat
when everything you eat comes from dark
and is drawn to the light you spread, and
nothing comes from the land you can see.

That night the blossoms bloomed at sea was
like so many nights our lads set the nets
and lit the diesel driven lights above them,
and the ever hungry water hissed beneath,
as the nets played out and the shrimp rose
drawn to an artificial dawn, and the great fish,
those that knew the eternal darkness of life,
rose to the light that filled their lidless eyes
and thrashed in the final spectacle of death
drawn to the elusive light that gave them life,
trapped thrashing into a world of demons.

The blossoms bloomed at sea distant while
I watched, first one and then an hour later another,
so that I held my girl in wonder on the beach
asking what was that and what was that, holding
each other's hands as we watched the fairy lights
those trawlers carried on their rigging burst,
becoming flames that lit those floating cities
on the beaches back in October of 1941. The next
day, that fast, the trawlers knew to dark their lights
but the bodies of some of our Town-folk came in
smelling of the world of commerce and of Europe
and their eyes like those of fish filled with memory.

We read then of the U-Boats off the coast of Coney
at night and the shape of freighters caught in the light
of amusement parks, and we learned to eat less
like the Great Depression that blew in from Arizona
and filled the sky over Washington. We were afraid,
but still Town is Town and you do what you must do.

Jared Smith

In the Heart of Town

They are in the heart of Town even now,
the deer trails that led from forest to streambed
that became the paths that predators knew so well
and then the moist earth trails of the first Americans
following the natural rolling contours of Earth
and then the dusty roads of wagon trains setting out
from Town into all those things that grow beyond.

They are the side-streets that cut across the grid,
the common paths that follow no plat lines but
follow instead into the hidden lives, bisecting highways
that have become the nation's paved neural network.
They are the birthplace of everything that is innocent
and everything that cries out in despair in the night,
and they are still the purveyors of what makes every town
its own time and place, its own music, its own laughter.

West 4th above the Bait Shop

Richard lives on West 4th Street above the bait shop.
He hates the flies that keep him awake all summer, hates
the way they see the world, hates their endless hunger but
he paints the town in excruciating detail in oils on wood,
brush strokes and palette knife gouging out and scraping
away the shadows, painting wide-eyed angels on street corners,
their faces worn and the shade of storm sails, eyes blood red
reaching out toward the viewer as he sees them every day,
their wings folded around their shoulders like woolen scarves,
their features the knotholes of old willows gone away.

We've had our share of talks because he knows something
about the history of mankind whether he's right or wrong
and I can hear the music beating in my head as he talks, and
the colors he uses, the pigments he pulls from the earth
are not like the ones they sell in artists' stores or schools.
I call him Dick, but quietly not to give offense because
he's a painter who paints with the land and has a harpoon
hanging on the wall behind his bed and talks with demons
no one else can see but we can't see the angels either and
their eyes reach out to us with all the pain we had forgotten
that separated us from each other and the stars at night.

Downstairs a heavy new flat of sandworms has been delivered.
Shiners are sweeping end to end in an arc across a metal tank,
their sides shimmering with the darkness of early morning,
catching the first rays of light gathering outside the windows
moving as one soul the door opens and a bell rings the door
closes and the voices of people begin to fill the air.

When a Town Fails

It's not always clear why a town fails.
In the West it may be that the gold gives out.
In New England or Georgia the lumber mills fail
with the old forests and not enough replanting.
In the Midwest it's the corn and drought or
nearer the cities it's the steel mills closing down,
the cars grinding to a halt in Detroit. Where
you build things of silicon, whether windows
or virtual realities that connect through fossil fuels,
usually it's an unforeseen weakness or weathering
a weak spot showing up in the infrastructure
where some executive slept too late one day
and failed to make his case to an indifferent board
or thought he had more suppliers or buyers than he did.
Or maybe it's something more perverse that gets him
or his most undervalued employee walks out the door.
Sometimes it's a stroke of luck, and sometimes a stroke
or just a matter of timing within eternity.

At some point the houses empty out and rodents
poke their way among the bricks, leaving droppings
that rustle dryly in the winds of summer, whiskers
set for finding food finding change instead, eyes
that take in the empty cupboards gods once filled,
rooms of gleaming corridors a maze in shadows,
and it's hard to get these things changed. It takes
a conversation, a murmur, a music in the background,
someone with no better place to be writing a new name
within a space that civilization has abandoned twice,
a creating of art that others hear of eventually and
a creative song that tells them how to breathe.

A Dove in Town

A dove, not collared, but spotted black,
dips below the fence line as a squirrel
makes its way between fruited mulberry
and an elm scraggly with its nest.

The path takes a hard right, barn wood
scarred with the sharpening of teeth.
A robin broadcasts three blue eggs.
The dove calls over and over,
worrying me before sleep.

Assembly of Birds in Town Say Leave

It was not just the dove that began to call to me,
but gulls and cardinals and red-winged blackbirds
from the reeds.

And you can't live on the sea without believing
in omens and signs and the periphery
that governs the mind.

I decided to take a winter job in Colorado—
second to allow women the vote—
at a college co-educational, liberal arts.

And south by a winding highway
was another town called Town, Pueblo,
on the once-border with Mexico.

The birds were right. Their calls more
than a herald to the change of seasons.
I would work at the foot of Pikes Peak,

teach theatre and dance, live forty
miles south as I did from Atlantic City .
This was meant as a gestation,

where I would spend nine months
every year, until I could return
to the lights and stage and dancing.

First Day of Summer in Town

You wake to the gentle lap of bay on shore—
coarse grass of dunes and sand littered
with seaweed and glass washed smooth,
green and brown of beer bottles, hardly any blue.

As temperatures rise, you switch to ocean,
waves more biting, the side of body leaned
into the crash tells not your strength,
but your weakness, what you're willing to risk.

Go west; live on the skirt of mountains.
Take their brunt; accept this embrace.
Find the gold in every prospector's tale at the bar.
Save this shack on Fishing Creek.

Looking for a Place in Western Town

The overnight train to Chicago gets in after eight a.m.
I have a sleeper, hang my clothes out for the conductor
to press. The Super Chief arrives the next morning
in La Junta, CO, then a quick change to a local line
to Pueblo, station backed up onto a levee, the Arkansas
River behind, West and water both unpredictable.

The bars on Union Avenue are busy even though
it isn't noon yet because of round-the-clock shifts
at the mill. And just so I know I'm in the West,
there's a hanging tree in the middle of the street.

Rooming houses advertise whether you get a bath or not.
I head north toward steeples I see from the top of the bridge,
to First Presbyterian, across from the Court House.
I ask at the office if anyone rents rooms.

"Try Elsie on Grand, religion teacher at Park Hill School."
I trudge thirteen blocks, sit with my bag at my feet.
A drug store fountain drink tastes good after heat
I could feel coming up through the soles of my shoes.

Elsie drives up in a Nash, bun so tight on her head
it pulls her eyes even wider seeing me on the porch.

"Euonymus mixed with privet?"
I ask about the hedge across the front walk.
"Now how do you know that?"
"Privet's not strong enough alone. Can you keep flowers
going past first frost in this courtyard you've got?"
"I can if you'll keep them watered."

Jared Smith

Windows

Windows are not built into walls
but perhaps between them seen and unseen
they are set in stone and placed in air
where faces will find them on winter days
or when the work hours have grown too long,
or sometimes they are formed of stained glass
and light will come into them to light those
lined up below with their hats off to glory,

but still you can tell a lot about a man
by the windows he is comfortable with
and what he likes to look upon at dawn
because some look like school houses
and others like prisons or factories or just
the kind of place you wouldn't throw stones

or windows are failed doors at times
meant for the ancient ones to enter and
left open until a people or time have failed,
but they still stare out across time and sunset
and perhaps the souls they were placed for
will return, count their credits, and move on.

Dancing in Atlantic City

The dancers' hotel down the street from Steel Pier
has transoms over the doors, a way for cool to get in,
create a cross breeze for windows open onto the narrow stretch
between buildings.

Conversations carry from one room to the next,
same as night voices of drink and gambling down the hall,
not many secrets kept. Members of the bands stay there too,
the Dorsey Brothers, Benny Goodman.

I only stay when the show runs late, too tired to drive home,
always get a room to myself, more cash than the rest
because I am almost a local, scorned by the dancers.
The transients couldn't have lasted the winters,

couldn't have overcome the isolation. But it stands me well.
Easier to say "no" to what gets the other girls in trouble,
Benzedrine for high kicks and smiles all down the line,
the heroin they use to come down.

Single rooms, late night swims, meals at small glass
fronted places off the boardwalk, early morning walks
that tone legs as your feet rock side to side in the sand,
afternoons under an umbrella to keep an even skin tone.

Nothing's worse than a sunburn under sequins and fishnet
stockings. Those of us around a season or two know how to pace
ourselves to Labor Day when the city folds up like the big black
trunks dancers live out of while on the road.

About Jared Smith

Jared Smith is the author of twelve volumes of poetry including his *Collected Poems: 1971-2011,* multimedia productions based on his poetry in New York and Chicago; two CDs; and numerous publications in the applied sciences. His poems, essays, and literary commentary have appeared in hundreds of publications in the U.S., Europe, and China. He is a Board Member of *The New York Quarterly Foundation* and is Poetry Editor of *Turtle Island Quarterly.* He has also served on the Editorial Boards of *The New York Quarterly, Home Planet News, The Pedestal,* and *Trail & Timberline.* He is listed in *Poets & Writers, The Colorado Poets Center, Who's Who in America,* and other major reference sources. Jared has three nominations for a Pushcart Prize.

Jared holds a Master's Degree in Literature from New York University and studied under *The Great Books Program* at St. John's College in Santa Fe. He has taught at New York University and La Guardia Community College (CCNY); and worked as a Director of Education and Research at Gas Technology Institute, as technical and policy adviser to several White House commissions under President William Clinton, and as Special Appointee to Argonne National Laboratory. He lives in the foothills of the Rockies. His website is *www.jaredsmith.info.*

About Kyle Laws

Kyle Laws' previous collections include *So Bright to Blind* (Five Oaks Press, 2015); *Wildwood* (Lummox Press, 2014); *George Sand's Haiti* (co-winner of Poetry West's 2012 award, published 2013); *My Visions Are As Real As Your Movies, Joan of Arc Says to Rudolph Valentino* (Dancing Girl Press, 2013); *Storm Inside the Walls* (Little Books Press, 2012); and *Going into Exile* (Abbey Chapbooks, 2012).

With five nominations for a Pushcart Prize, her poems and essays have appeared in magazines and anthologies in the U.S., U.K., and Canada. She is the editor of Casa de Cinco Hermanas Press and a member of Arts Alliance Studios Community, Pueblo, CO. Her website is *www.kylelaws.com*.

Acknowledgments

- Jared Smith's poems, "That Night in '41" and "West 4th above the Bait Shop," have previously appeared in the *Malpaís Review*.

- Jared Smith's poem, "Turner Bay," has previously appeared in *Paterson Literary Review*.

- Jared Smith's poem, "The Salt Marshes," has previously appeared in *The Same* as well as in *Lyrical Somerville*.

- Jared Smith's poems, "How Do You Look at This Space?" and "In the Heart of Town," have appeared in the *Turtle Island Quarterly*.

- Kyle Laws' poems, "This Town," "Why Would Anyone Want to Live in Town?" and "Dancing in Atlantic City," have previously appeared in the *Malpaís Review*.

- Kyle Laws' poem, "When I First Came to Town, the Only Business," has previously appeared in *Verse Osmosis*.

Other Books from Liquid Light Press

All Liquid Light Press books are available directly from *liquidlightpress.com* or from any of the current major global distribution channels including Amazon, Barnes and Noble, the iBookstore and the Ingram Catalog.

- ♥ *Leaning Toward Whole* by M. D. Friedman (2011) — Explores the poignant and personal. Also available as a groundbreaking multimedia enhanced e-book.
- ♥ *The Miracle Already Happening — Everyday Life with Rumi* by Rosemerry Wahtola Trommer (2011) — A special collection of poems full of heart, humor, peace and wisdom.
- ♥ *Spiral* by Lynda La Rocca (2012) — A compelling poetic and melodic discourse of the persistent cravings and fears inside of each of us.
- ♥ *From the Ashes* by Wayne A. Gilbert (2012) — A true masterpiece that gnaws at the heart with universal appeal.
- ♥ *ah* by Rachel Kellum (2012) — This poetry has a simplicity and clarity that cuts to the core of being human.
- ♥ *Catalyst* by Jeremy Martin (2012) — *Catalyst* may just launch you on a fiery ride into yourself.
- ♥ *Of Eyes and Iris* by Erika Moss Gordon (2013) — Beautiful yet poignant in its simplicity.
- ♥ *Your House Is Floating* by Susan Whitmore (2013) — As smooth, crisp and satisfying as olive oil on fresh garden greens.
- ♥ *Nowhere Near Morning* by Jeffrey M. Bernstein (2013) — An intimate embrace of what it means to be alive.
- ♥ *Harmonica* by Cecele Allen Kraus (2014) — *Harmonica* bristles with a shimmering music that heals the heart.
- ♥ *Surf Sounds* by Roger Higgins (2014) — Expertly crafted and superbly written, pulsing with the tides of the soul.
- ♥ *Black-Footed Country* by Lindsay Wilson (2015) — Like eating an artichoke, there are layers within thorny layers, each one more tender and subtle until you feast on the heart inside.
- ♥ *The Dice Throwers* by Douglas Cole (2015) — *The Dice Throwers* shines like a flashlight across the gritty dark alleys of the American soul, turning shattered glass into diamonds.
- ♥ *Lessons on Sleeping Alone* by Megan E. Freeman (2015) — While easily accessible, Megan's elegant writing is complexly layered with hard-won common sense and clarity.
- ♥ *The Offering* by Eleanor Kedney (2016) — A masterful, poetic tapestry woven from what makes us human.